A Thousand Words of Poetry

Karla Matson

Presentation by *BookLeaf Publishing*

Web: www.bookleafpub.com

E-mail: info@bookleafpub.com

ISBN: 9789395621083

First edition 2022

Bluebird

Bluebird singing
At the peak of day
Take flight on energetic wing
Flight so swift to far away.

Nature's Strength

I hope you are blessed
with the strength of nature,
To endure as the might oak,
and bend as the willows do.
To grow as the wildflowers after
being trampled.
And provide as berry bushes can while
weathering the worst of summer storms,
and flourish as lush grass,
even in the most desolate and broken grounds.

Spring to Summer

Springtime air at dusk
Signals approaching change comes
Summer arrives

Bloom

4

Budding flowers
Soft in green leaves abound here
Dainty scent perfume

Dawn

5

Golden glory shifts
At dawn in transformation
Break of a new day

Kintsugi

Soul held in parts past repair,
Thought in despair.
Broken, battered, damaged,
There is still life to be managed.
Heed this, yet still darkness,
Lie no starkness.
Fill to brim and yield veins of gold,
Shine and cracks rebuilt to hold.

Vow

I vow this to you,
I swear by all mine love and passion within,
To speak truth,
Touch with tender lingering caress,
Stare into eyes so vivid,
I swear by all blood within,
To wipe away every tear,
And kiss upon laughing lips,
I swear to hold you for all time,
And stay with you to love til the end of me.

Heart

Shine and burnish oft
Heart made of steel and with gold
Forever loved on

Urge

Some days
I feel more spirit
than flesh and I gaze
Earnestly at the glittering stars,
suppressing the urge to join
and soar with them.

Celestial

She danced on colours of rainbow prism
Wings of stardust alight
Crowned in golden halo

Laughter adrift upon breath of mistral
Voice sublime music note upon the ear
Eyes bright and nebular

Dewdrops gather to pearlized in lustrous locks
Gossamer gauze swirls translucent silk
Exquisite vision, intangible to touch

Haunting memory
Her entity celestial

Phantasm

Harken the abyssal ere midnight
Passing zephyr a tender brush to skin
Lo, scarce is the will-o-the-wisp light
Ephemeral as the melody of haunting song to
kin

No Escape

So weary and unable to go on
I cannot continue to pretend
Suffocating, supressed by my fears
I cannot reach to see the light

Your face still lingers in the shadows
Its beauty haunting my dreams
Your constant memory hurts
I'm bound by the scars you left behind

I tried so hard to convince myself you're gone
But though I know the truth
Your hand still holds mine captured
There's too much that time cannot erase

These wounds just won't heal within
The pain is far too real
No matter how far I run
I can never escape you

Prophecy

Whisper of voices; mysterious
Threads of unknown
Cascade together, enacting harmony as one
Compelling to what is now known

Passing shadow tainting the brilliant moon
One shall bring destruction
Possessed in evil untold

He shall seek blood of balance
Sleeping in darkness, awaiting the time
Power long forgotten, given to rest
Rise of the Demons

Wait for the Descent into new beginnings
Child of magic
Born creation of darkness
Marked by prophecy
Time of the rising will bring destruction and
peace

Return to what once was; begin anew
Sacrifice to bring to others Hope
Light to Darkness, male to female
Guardians shall endure to See the ending

Rise of magic
Connect all threads
Element calls to element, dreams beckon to
another
Seek the lost ones
Lure the Children home to her

Resurrection of old shall bring forgotten secrets
New strength found shall open new doors to
choose
Blood marks the land in death, kills haunting in
both worlds
Beware the Rogue of Mortality

Autumn

Sun radiating through haze of fog
Steamed past yawing branches spread
Gold alight upon colours of lurid, amber, and
crimson
Earthy scent at end of season
Frost threatens as air transitions to brisk

Clock

Tik, Tik comes the chime
Tok, Tok dongs the grandfather
Cuckoo sings the clock

Fire

17

Warmth radiates out
Red, yellow and hint of blue
Strike created fire

Happy

Sunshine, books, and hugs
A day with quiet and smiles
Happiness lingers

Edge

Tipping point on edge
Faded, weathered and at risk
Journey completed

Love

I love you
Obsessively,
Irrationally, in consuming passion
Ringing, resounding, reverberating
Ache deep, pining
With maddening hunger of eager,
hot desire

Do Not Cry for Me

Do not cry for me ere
Though you cannot see
Nothing remains to share
I am with you wild and free

Never do I sleep
I am the thousand voices on the winds that blow
Engraved upon the seas of deep
And in the glittering crystals of mountain snow

I am the warm sunlight upon colourful
wildflowers
And the pattering drops of rainfall
When you wake in early morning hours
Seeking a hushed familiar call

I am the unerring serenity of a lullaby song
Hummed gently under grace of the moonlight
I am the pulse within you so strong
And beckoning with the twinkle that shines from
stars at night

Do not cry for me ere
Though you cannot see
Nothing remains to share
I am with you wild and free

Two Roads

22

Two roads to travel
Split to part in opposite
One easy, one not